JELLY SIDE UP!

MARY J. PRYOR

Copyright 1997 by Mary J. Pryor
Illustrations copyright 1997 by Donna Carpenter

All rights reserved.
No part of this book may be used or reproduced
in any manner whatsoever
without written permission from the author.

Published by
Old Rivers Press
P.O. Box 851435
Yukon, OK 73085
(405) 354-1604

First Printing–November, 1997

Printed in the United States of America

Library of Congress Catalog Number: 97-92619

ISBN:1-887587-01-2

for my Mom . . .

Table of Contents

Welcome to Jelly Side Up 6

Chapter 1: Buttoning Up 13

Chapter 2: Seven Days in a Week 27

Chapter 3: Do It Now 39

Chapter 4: Stay in the Beanstalks 55

Chapter 5: Big Frogs 67

Chapter 6: All the Possibilities 81

Chapter 7: First Aid for Jelly Down Days 95

April 26, 1997

>As I start to write this book, I'm at my desk
>>–with a cup of good coffee
>>–all my writing stuff
>>–and a big bowl of strawberries.

Now, the first and third things on that list might not be necessary for this book, but they are making it more fun to write. The strawberries are from California, those huge red ones we get here in Oklahoma only in the spring. And they're fresh.

My refrigerator is full of flats of strawberries too pretty to be believed–except one flat that's pretty picked over. Because its best berries are in front of me now.

I plan to enjoy them. They're my current object lesson in finding time–for what's important in my life. That's what I wish for you too–the time for the things important to you.

I've no shortage of what I'd like to do,
—with my time,
—with my life.

I've got projects, piles, and ideas,
and lots of things in the categories of
*I want to/need to,
hope I can find time for,
and when I'm not too busy I'm going to . . .*

Not very different from you, you say?
There never will be time for everything I want to do, but there really is enough time for everything that's important.

Here's an old saying—
*The only way
to assure your bread will end
jelly side up on the floor
is to put jelly*
on both sides.

And that's what this book is about.

Getting your bread to land jelly side up—
all the time.

Getting what you want from your life.

Having time for what
you want to do,

and finding time for what's important
in *your* life.

Of course, you do that every day—find time
for the important things in your life. Don't you?
Your community, your job, your home,
your friends, your hobbies, your passions.
But sometimes, in finding time for all of those,
we find there's not enough time for ourselves.

Are you good at that—making or finding time for
others, and not finding time for yourself?

Don't feel alone.
We are many.

Why is it so easy to see when someone else needs you? Why is it so hard to help yourself, to find time to grow, renew, recharge, and feel good about all of your choices?

None of us want to just cover the bases, get things done, cross things off our lists. We want to feel good about doing things that satisfy deeply.

You want time to do the things that give you great enjoyment, things that make you feel happy, fulfilled, and pleased with your life. You want time to do the things that let you relax and accomplish long-standing dreams.

When you think about it, jelly is a lot like life. It's colorful, rich, and comes in many varieties.

It tastes good!

It's wonderful.

It's bright.

It can get sticky.

Like life, jelly can be spread too thin. And then it doesn't taste as good. But you get to choose how little or how much to use!

The Jelly Side Up Philosophy of Finding Time For What's Important In Your Life (hereinafter referred to simply as Jelly Side Up) addresses this most important issue, and gives you at least sixty ways! to find time for what's important to you.

Notice I didn't say easy ways. Sometimes it may be, some things might not. But it's not the point to find an easy, fast way to fix how you feel about not having time for what's important. Because if there was such a way, you and I would have already found it.

The point is
to think about, decide,
and make some important changes
that allow you to find time for:

This space for all the things that are important to you. Write very small.

Got the point? Very good. Read on. This book is about feeling better about the ways you choose to use your time.

It's about job satisfaction.
It's about life satisfaction.

It's about reflecting on what you're currently doing, your level of involvement, your finished and unfinished projects, and feeling that the trade-off in time, energy, and commitment is worth it.

It's about finding time
for the results you want.

If you've ever said, *That was worth every second I spent on it. If I had to do it over, I wouldn't change a thing. I'm that happy with the result.* then you've experienced finding time for what's important in your life.

So, if you're looking for completely new information, something you've never heard or read before—it's probably not in this book.

What you will find in these pages however, are ideas that can change your life.

If you let them.

If you're ready, committed, and open to change, Jelly Side Up! can help you find time for the results you want. If you're ready, you can *increase the time you have* for what's important in your life.

*You may not get
what you want in life,
but in the long run,
you will get what you expect.*
—Denis Waitley

What This Book Is Not

It's not a quick fix.
It's not full of easy choices.
It's not work someone else can do for you.
It's 'work' that will make you think and choose, and perhaps make some decisions that can affect your life–starting right now.

*In life,
I've been done in
more by the drips
than the floods.*

❖ 1 ❖

The First
Jelly Principle

Once you've missed the first buttonhole, you will have trouble buttoning up.

IDENTIFY YOUR PRIORITIES.

There's a great cartoon that addresses the point of having a system. It shows a sleepy, groggy, disheveled man who's just gotten out of bed.

He's staring at the wall and there's a poster on the wall that says:

> FIRST YOUR PANTS,
> AND THEN YOUR SHOES.

While that doesn't have much to do with jelly, bread, or your life, it does point out that there is something worthwhile, some merit in doing the important first things first.

Button The First Button
Identify Your Priorities

Clearly defined priorities
will assure that you find time
for the important things.
Without clearly defined priorities,
you and I focus on activity.

Well, everybody knows their high priorities.

Oh, really?

Right now, *write down the three things you value most in life.*

On paper.
Right here on this page.
You need to see this.

1.

2.

3.

Now look at those three things. Next to each one, put the honest amount of time you spent on each one in the last two weeks.

There is significance in including what you've done in the last two weeks. Every week doesn't let you and I work toward our priorities. Sometimes some get shoved aside, buried for a day or two, or eaten alive by the gremlins.

But in two weeks–that would be two times a month–if it's important to you, if it's a priority, then there should be *a significant amount of time spent on these things you value so highly.*

If you spent no time on these things, they weren't priority items.

Look at what you've written. Does the time spent reflect how important those things are to you? Looking at what you've written and the time spent on each priority, are you shocked, embarrassed, humbled, puzzled?

Welcome to the club.

You are not alone. You know where you'd *like* your priorities to be. Maybe in the last two weeks, you just haven't been able to find time for what's important in your life.

*Either you let your life slip away
by not doing the things you want to do,
or you get up and do them.*

A small amount of time spent on your priorities doesn't mean you don't value these things. You do!

It might mean, however, that you have trouble making those things the real priorities in your life.

Think about last week. It probably was a good reflection of some things that you identified and acted on as high priorities.

Last week probably also reflected some things that made themselves high priorities–like working late, taking on extra responsibilities, catching up, maintaining the status quo or meeting the needs of others.

You did what you did last week for very good reasons. But the things that you did, important as they were, may not be reflections of your life's priorities at all.

*Life is what happens
when you're making other plans.*

Are those your life priorities back on page fifteen?

If not, what do you want them to be?

What gives you the most enjoyment,

the deepest satisfaction?

What gives you that feeling of achievement

and well-being?

That's them!

*But I know
my priorities,
it's just
that the last two weeks . . .*

Someone somewhere is saying that, and finishing the sentence with:

> *my life has been crazy.*
>
> *my schedule was shot to pieces.*
>
> *I had to do it that way, I had no other choice.*

Ask yourself these questions

- ❖ What are you so busy on right now?
- ❖ What's so crucial in your life right now?
- ❖ What's taking up your time?
- ❖ What's using up your energy?

It's often the work overload, the everyday distractions, the added responsibilities that cause you to concentrate on them, *not on the end results* which make you feel so good about the way your time is spent.

*I've got my priorities,
but I also have to work for a living!*

Someone somewhere is saying that too.

Put It In Perspective

Your work is important, but maybe not for the reasons you think. Look again at the list you made. The things you do, the things that make a difference aren't the deadlines you meet or the profit that you make.

I'll cheerfully refund what you paid for this book if I'm wrong, but I'm betting that your list reflects what you really do–value people. I'm betting that it exhibits what's important to you, and that it reflects your philosophy of life.

I'm betting that every item on that list reflects a good choice on your part, and that's why those items made the list. I'm also betting that some of these things are the things that frustrate you.

*In my life there have been no dragons.
Only small spiders
and stepped-in chewing gum.
I could have handled dragons.*

*If you take good care of the moment,
the years will take care of themselves.*
—John-Roger & Peter McWilliams

It's hard to see value, direction, or possible results when you're distracted, overworked, and stressed. That is also the time you need to see your priorities very clearly.

Ways To Discover Priorities

- ❖ Talk it out.

    You'll be surprised what you hear.
- ❖ Write it out.

    The answers may surprise you.
- ❖ Make a list, whittle it down.
- ❖ Look around you.

    What surrounds you?
- ❖ Peruse your calendar.
- ❖ Look at your checkbook.

    Where does the money go?

pri•or•i•ty *n.*
1. precedence in time, order, importance, 2. the first buttonhole you must not miss.

Where could you be in one year if you gave your high priorities one hour a day? There's power in investment.

If you're not spending an hour a day on your goals, what *are* you doing?

LONG, LONG LISTS OF PRIORITIES . . .

are not a good thing! A long list makes it look like everything in life is a priority, and that can't be. If everything shouts

HIGH PRIORITY

that's a warning sign. It may mean you have difficulty prioritizing between work and personal life, making the most important important, or sticking with a course of action.

The First Jelly Principle is the best tool you have. It puts something right at your side that can help you decide what to do, what not to do, whether to say yes or no to requests for your time, money, and energy.

And now, time for a commercial break.

Here's a good book.

Life 101
Everything We Wish We Had Learned About Life In School—But Didn't
by John-Roger and Peter McWilliams

As the L.A. Times said, "The title jolly well says it all."

At the fork in the road,

Alice asked the Cheshire Cat which road to take.

The Cheshire Cat asked,

"Where do you want to go?"

To which Alice replied, "I don't know."

"Then," said the Cat,

"It doesn't matter which way you go."

—LEWIS CARROLL
ALICE IN WONDERLAND

When you know your priorities and use them as a decision making tool, you're using a life management technique called *Rule In / Rule Out*.

It works like this:
- ❖ It's Saturday.
- ❖ You want to sleep in.
- ❖ One friend wants to shop for furniture.
- ❖ You ought to go visit your mother.
- ❖ The house is overdue for a good cleaning.
- ❖ You'd like to run all your errands.
- ❖ There's another friend you want to see.

Make that your Saturday just for a moment. Look at the list and decide which of those items reflect your priorities.

More than one probably. But which one, if you chose it, would wordlessly be a testimony of what's important in your life? Which action would cause someone to say, *Wow, that must really be important to you.*

IF IT'S IMPORTANT
IT TAKES PRECEDENCE.
―――――――――――

You *rule in* the most important, and *rule out* everything else, at least for now. The First Jelly Principle helps you pick the best of a bunch of good choices.

*You can't have everything.
Where would you put it?*

Using Rule In/Rule Out takes care of the things you think you should do. The have tos, the musts and the shoulds are ruled out, because they don't relate to your highest priorities. (Those were excellent berries.)

*If your goals
are written, prioritized, and worked,
then your time is protected.*

Over time, if you use Rule In/Rule Out, you'll find it easier to make choices and you'll find more time for the things you really value.

❖

Knowing Is Not Doing

We know about putting First Things First, If It Is To Be It's Up To Me, the One Minute Manager.

We *know* a lot, but what we *do* with what we know is a different story. That may be why priorities seem out of sync with the time spent on them.

It's easy to say, *This is important to me.*
It's hard, hard, hard to let that importance
be reflected in behavior, decisions, and the ways
we use our time.

The truth of the matter

is that you always know

the right thing to do.

The hard part is doing it.
—GENERAL H. NORMAN SCHWARZKOPF

Knowing buttons up
no buttonholes.

Knowing
puts no jelly on either side of the bread.

It is hard to fight an enemy
who has outposts in your head.
—SALLY KEMPTON

Don't Miss That First Buttonhole

❖ Let your priorities make your choices.

❖ Use Rule In/Rule Out to make decisions.

❖ Realize you can't do everything.
   Well, at least not today!

❖ 2 ❖
THE SECOND
Jelly Principle

Someday is not a day of the week.

CREATIVE AVOIDANCE
WHY SOME OF US NEVER GET THE JELLY ON THE BREAD AT ALL.

Jelly Principle #1
Once you miss the first buttonhole, you will have trouble buttoning up.

Jelly Principle #2
Someday is not a day of the week.

There's a strong force at work when you decide on a course of action. Like your New Year's resolutions, you're filled with energy.

>Start a degree program!
>Save $500 a month!
>Exercise every day!
>Lose 15 pounds!

There is commitment at the beginning of any new endeavor. Chances are though, you'll reach a point when you come up with some very good *reasons* why you really didn't want to do something anyway. And you will have some very, very, very good reasons.

Think of the last time this happened to you, and the reasons you had for altering your original course of action.

This changing your mind isn't changing your mind at all. It's an example of your wonderful creative brain practicing *creative avoidance*.

A Definition

>Deciding against a course of action
>by imagining that the disadvantages
>outweigh the benefits.

People really do creatively avoid situations. And here's why. You and I have good reasons—money, or lack of it, time, kids, family responsibilities, friends, weather, mood. We can easily tell someone or ourselves why we're not taking action—yet.

Once we've stated our reasons, then we can stop, quit, go back to what we were doing before. And we can continue to say, *Someday . . .*

*Someday is not
the eighth day of the week.*

Someday means, *I've decided this is too complex, new, frightening, unfamiliar, or not important enough, and so I'm going back to what I know. I'm going back to what is familiar and comfortable.* It's also going back to something easier, and maybe something less important.

Creative avoidance is a movement away from an object or goal by means of the imagination with the intent of anxiety reduction. Procrastination is one way to creatively avoid a situation.

–Lou Tice

*A person who aims at
nothing
has a target he can't miss.*

You and I go back to the familiar and the known. Because it is! It doesn't take so much energy, or time, or hard thinking. I've lived in the comfortable and familiar a long time. I like it there. It's predictable and it's safe.

❖

*When it comes to guilt trips,
I'm a frequent flyer.*

Don't put on your exercise clothes. This is not the time for you to take an activity break and beat yourself up for things you have or haven't done. You are entitled to every choice you make. Judging yesterday's choices by where you are today is pointless. You're not at that place. This is today, not yesterday.

*I realized early on that success
was tied to not giving up.
Most people in this business gave up
and went on to other things.
If you simply didn't give up,
you would outlast the people
who came in on the bus with you.*
—Harrison Ford

And now, the world class excuses . . .
Take a moment and think about your best ones. You know, the ones you say are reasons, the ones that are so strong. The ones that keep popping up inside your head as you're reading. Think of the things you'd really like to tell me— why this stuff may not work for you.

Now, read my money-back guarantee:

You will move toward those things you think about.

And if you don't, you'll be the first person in the world who ever managed to think one way and act another!

My brain does a good job manufacturing excuses for me to use. It even convinces me that they're not excuses at all, they're reasons! And my brain is so good, these excuses look like the best of reasons. It's not called creative avoidance for nothing!

So, what's the problem? My reasons or excuses keep me in the someday mode. And that means I'll never do anything that I've said I would do *someday.*

*If you don't get started,
you won't get finished.*
—Unknown

None of us want to spend less time or energy on what's important. That's not the problem. The problem is biting off too much to chew, getting into unfamiliar territory, being around too much new too fast. That's when we say, *Well, maybe not just now. Maybe someday.* We've moved back to what we know. We'll do this every time that the familiar is clearer to us than the future.

*You always move toward
your strongest picture.*
—Lou Tice

Meet The Poverty Mentality

Here is the thought process that convinces you there's never enough to go around. Makes for handy excuses. Such as, *There's not enough time, so I can't work on the important things now. They'll have to wait.*

When we operate from a poverty mentality, you and I assume there's not enough. So we find ourselves saying,

Well, maybe someday . . .

❖

*We can always choose
to perceive things differently.
You can focus on what's wrong in your life,
or you can focus on what's right.
But whatever you focus on,
you're going to get more of.
Creation is an extension of thought.
Think lack, and you get lack.
Think abundance, and you get more.*
—Marianne Williamson

When you come from the idea of never enough—as in: *I don't have enough time.*

There are too many interruptions in my life.

There's not enough money for that now.

I don't have the background to do that.

there never will be enough. Remember, you move toward the things you think about. You're not really serious about moving toward interruptions, crowded time, depleted budgets, and no experience. Are you?

If the horse is dead, dismount.
—Jim Fitzpatrick

Did this ever work? When did statements like those at the top of this page ever make you feel better, earn you more, increase your happiness?

*Pitcher Tom Seaver once asked Yogi Berra
what time it was.
Yogi's reply was, "You mean now?"*

*It's not
what you are
that holds you back,
it's what you think
you are not.*

What bogs you down? That's where your energy goes. Put some thought into this. You'll need an answer by Chapter Three. More later.

> *Fatigue makes cowards of us all.*
> —Vince Lombardi

To get someday out of your week and out of your life

- ❖ bite off tiny bites.
- ❖ make baby contracts.
- ❖ stick to something ten minutes longer.
- ❖ try something just one more time.
- ❖ make the future your strongest picture.
- ❖ ask yourself how you'll feel if you don't continue this course of action.

The longer I live the more I realize
the impact of attitude on life.
Attitude to me is more important than facts.
It is more important than the past, than education,
than money, than circumstances, than failures,
than successes, than what other people think or say or do.
It is more important than appearance, giftedness or skill.
It will make or break a company, a church, a home.
The remarkable thing is we have a choice every day
regarding the attitude we embrace for that day.
We cannot change our past, we cannot change the fact
that people will act in a certain way.
We cannot change the inevitable.
The only thing we can do
is play on the one string we have,
and that is our attitude.
I am convinced that life is
ten percent what happens to me
and ninety percent how I react to it.
And as it is with you.
We are in charge of our attitude.
—CHARLES SWINDOLL

Jelly Principle #1
Once you miss the first buttonhole, you will have trouble buttoning up.

Jelly Principle #2
Someday is not a day of the week.

Jelly Principle #3
Time flies like an arrow.
Fruit flies like a banana.

❖ 3 ❖

The Third
Jelly Principle

**Do It Now.
Bread Only Lands Jelly Side Up
When You Stop Wasting Time.**

Everybody has a system.
Let me tell you about my piles.

I have

project piles,

Not Today piles,

got to order from piles,

pay these bills piles,

stuff that needs

looking at again piles,

and the

projects

too big

to start on today piles . . .

Well, you get the idea. My life sometimes piles up on top of me, and *Do It Now!* is a phrase that causes me a great deal of frustration. I have a lot of responses when my mind asks, *Are we going to do something about all those piles?*

Want to hear my creative responses? I have few of those. But I have a lot of really old familiar whiny lines:

I know, I know, I will.
I'm going to, but first . . .
Anytime but this week.
Look at my schedule and you'll understand.
Do it now is easy for you to say!

Not very original, are they?
But they work.
They keep the eighth day in my week.
They totally ignore the fact that time keeps flying while I keep putting things off.

My sister Tricia lives five hundred miles from me. One day on the phone we were lamenting how much we had to do. We started talking about all the things that had piled up and were waiting for us to do something about them. Tricia was at that point, recognizable to a lot of us, when something *has* to be done.

"I don't know where to start," she said. "There are nine separate piles on my dining room table right now."

It would have been funny, except that, at times, the number of my piles far exceeds nine.

Change will come only when the pain of staying the same is greater than the pain of change.

That day, Tricia had reached that point. Her stress level was high enough. She was ready to move.

Get A Handle On Things

I keep my promises. This is Chapter Three, so let me ask you again. What bogs you down? Where does your energy go?

If you can't find the problem, you can't fix it. And your answers *are* important because what ties you up, may tie up your energy too.

We've all had those days when someone asked, "What did you do today?" and we couldn't remember doing much at all! A common response is *I know I was busy, but I can't think of one thing I got done.*

It happens more frequently than we'd like. It happens all the time when you're wrapped up in trivia.

Another one of my famous guarantees!
If your day is devoted to trivia,
you'll have little recall of any satisfying activity,
because trivia is never satisfying.

It's frustrating knowing or feeling I really didn't get much accomplished today. It adds to the stress in my life, and I'm not looking for that kind of an addition.

Your job and mine come complete with enough stress. Or, as Malcolm Forbes said, If you have a job without aggravation, you don't have a job.

Time For A Test

1. How often do you *Do It Now*?

2. How much time do you waste?

3. How much stress does this create?

It's a cycle. Put something off, perhaps do something trivial instead, (something valuable like reading your junk mail) worry about what should be getting done–get stressed–worry because my stress level is high–decide there are things I can or can't do because I'm currently stressed.

The stress builds. It becomes harder and harder to break away from that cycle. Stress is a fact of life, but too much stress means the jelly doesn't even get spread on the bread, and that takes the joy out of life.

The truth of the matter?
People waste far more emotional energy
desperately hanging on to old habits and beliefs
than it would take
for them to embrace the changes.
—Price Pritchett and Ron Pound

Successful People Do Things Differently

- ❖ Successful people don't go home depleted.
- ❖ They work faster, at times.
- ❖ They value personal time the most.
- ❖ They surround themselves with upbeat people.
- ❖ They are farsighted.
- ❖ They don't waste your time or mine.
- ❖ They're open to different approaches.
- ❖ They're relaxed.
- ❖ They turn to friends for advice.
- ❖ They can separate the critical few from the trivial many.

Looking at that list, count the actions you own. How many were reflected in your day? Own your successes!

Your living is determined not so much

by what life brings to you

as by the attitude you bring to life,

not so much by what happens to you

as by the way your mind looks at what happens.

Circumstances and situations do color your life,

but you have been given the mind to choose

what the color shall be.
—John Homer Miller

Remember Rule In/Rule Out? It can help you Do It Now! It can focus you on the priorities and give you a handle on the trivia that edges into your day and consumes your energy.

Using your priorities to make decisions on what to Do Now decreases stress, increases satisfaction, builds strong bones . . . well, maybe two of the three.

Do It Now—Reduce The Stress

Successful people recognize timewasters. Dr. Jan Yager says those are:

- spreading yourself too thin
- being afraid to delegate
- not wanting to say no
- being a slave to the phone
- procrastination

Hmm—care to choose one of your favorites? Sometimes doing it now releases energy you've tied up. Sometimes doing it now generates the positive energy you need. Sometimes doing it now creates more energy than you thought you had.

When you decide you can't find time for what's important in your life, you will be momentarily reducing stress, but the stress will still be there. Over time, it may even increase.

You internally generate your own stress.

By choosing what to do or not do, by rationalizing, by settling for a less than satisfactory solution, you build stress. The bread doesn't land jelly side up. The danger signs are easy to see.

Tight muscles, a stomach that's tied in knots, headaches that happen a little too frequently, feeling rushed, depleted, burning from a short fuse . . .

That's internally generated stress. It works against *doing it now*. It builds even more stress.

*You're entitled to your own opinions.
You are not entitled
to your own facts.*
—UNKNOWN

There are three things that distinguish a stressbusting thought from its evil twin, the stress builder:

❖ A stressbusting statement will never contain the word not. As in *I'm not going to feel so stressed tomorrow.*

❖ A stressbusting statement is personal and is always stated in the first person singular. As in *I control stress with daily exercise.*

❖ A stressbusting statement is always in the present tense. As in *I rule in what's important*, not *I'm going to start working on my stress level.*

Your helpful subconscious mind doesn't hear *not*. It does understand who *me, my* and *I* are, and it only acts on things stated in the present tense. Make your self-talk positive, personal, and present tense. There's no time attached to *I'm going to, I plan to . . .* Your helpful subconscious will never bother you with things that you don't plan to do now.

> *Being extremely honest with one's self is a good exercise.*
> —UNKNOWN

It may help to picture yourself as you look and act in peaceful situations. What's so neat about the peaceful you? Are you smiling? relaxed? unhurried? taking time to make decisions?

This is the person you need to see when the stress is building. It may be helpful to make a mental list of the words describing this person. That way, even if you can't see the peaceful you clearly, you can always describe that person– *peaceful, calm, relaxed, happy, finding time for what's important.*

Babior and Goldman call this the Rational You. Rational means smart, you know.

Julie White has a great technique to put you in touch with this Rational You. She suggests imagining a conversation with your kindest relative, an aunt perhaps. What would she say to you in a stressful situation? What would she recommend or advise?

White also suggests you might think of a coach, a motivating person whose advice you value. What would a coach say? Would he encourage you to get moving? stay focused? keep your eyes on the goal?

Here's another good resource.

Image and Self Projection
For Today's Professional Woman

—Dr. Julie White
Career Track Publications

This woman is a wonder!

Identify your stressors, listen to your own good advice and *use* the techniques you've identified. Go ahead, leap! As Fred Bross says, they can't take away your birthday.

*"There's no use trying," said Alice.
"One can't believe impossible things."
"I dare say you haven't much practice,"
said the Queen. "When I was your age,
I always did it for half an hour a day.
Why, sometimes, I've believed as many as
six impossible things before breakfast."*
—LEWIS CARROLL
ALICE IN WONDERLAND

GET A HANDLE ON TIME

If you find yourself postponing this, give yourself a Do Better Talk. Meredith McClain swears by them. Follow the talk with just one Feel Better Activity. Do just one thing every day, no matter how small. It can be as serious and involved as taking a walk, smelling the flowers, cleaning the refrigerator. But do it, and do it consciously. Make it your decision.

At the risk of repeating myself . . .
Sometimes doing it now releases energy you've tied up. Sometimes doing it now generates the positive energy you need. Sometimes doing it now creates more energy than you thought you had.

*If you make a difference
with what you have,
you will see that it will expand.
And I'm talking about love,
I'm talking about time,
I'm talking about relatedness—
I'm even talking about money.
So when you make a difference with your life,
with your time, with your money, it expands,
and you don't have that focus on scrambling
to get more of what you don't really need,
which is what we're so busy doing
that we don't even notice who we are
and what we have.
And that is the context of sufficiency:
making a difference with who you are,
what you have, and knowing
that it's whole, complete and exactly enough.
It's perfection.*

—Lynne Twist

*If you want to strengthen your hand,
take time to shuffle the cards.*
—James R. Sherman

Successful People
Do Things Differently
And
Places To Start

- Congratulate yourself on what you do.

- Reward yourself.

- Experiment with talking to yourself.

- Keep a journal for a while.

- Most importantly, find the energy and *do it now*.

JELLY PRINCIPLE #1
ONCE YOU MISS THE FIRST BUTTONHOLE,
YOU WILL HAVE TROUBLE BUTTONING UP.

JELLY PRINCIPLE #2
SOMEDAY IS NOT A DAY OF THE WEEK.

JELLY PRINCIPLE #3
TIME FLIES LIKE AN ARROW.
FRUIT FLIES LIKE A BANANA.

JELLY PRINCIPLE #4
IF YOU ARE GOING TO KILL GIANTS,
YOU MUST SPEND YOUR TIME
IN THE BEANSTALKS,
NOT IN THE PEA VINES.

❖ 4 ❖

THE FOURTH
Jelly Principle

If you are going to kill giants, you must spend your time in the beanstalks, not in the pea vines.

YOU CAN'T CHANGE
IF YOU STAY WHERE YOU ARE.
SUCCESSFUL PEOPLE DO THINGS DIFFERENTLY.

Successful People Revisited

Just a gentle reminder, because it's easy to get tangled in the pea vines. Successful you . . .

- ❖ doesn't go home from work depleted.

- ❖ values your personal time the most.

- ❖ surrounds yourself with upbeat people.

- ❖ is farsighted.

- ❖ flexs enough to use different approaches.

- ❖ turns to friends for advice.

- ❖ works faster, at times.

- ❖ separates the critical from the trivial.

Uh-Oh! Potholes and Pitfalls

This is the danger zone. Sure there are a lot of things that can go wrong. Between the jelly and the bread. The best intentions and plans sometimes can't stand up to one of your more challenging days. It is the challenging days, however, when you really need to stay in the beanstalks.

WHAT YOU ACCOMPLISH IS DIRECTLY PROPORTIONAL TO THE TIME YOU SPEND IN THE BEAN PATCH.

In *Thinking Big*, Brian Tracy explains how tunnel vision keeps you from being where you want to be.

Tracy says you constrain yourself when you look too closely at your life. It's like holding your hand in front of your face, it's too close for you to notice anything except your hand. You can't see anything except the details.

You're constrained by the small stuff, by being too close to the problem.

When you're that close, you may have no perspective at all.

You may even be thinking, *I just don't see anything I can change or do differently.*

*Every now and then—go away.
Have a little relaxation.
For when you come back to your work,
your judgement will be surer,
since to remain constantly at work
will cause you to lose the power of judgement.
Go some distance away,
because then the work appears smaller—
and more of it can be taken in at a glance,
and a lack of harmony or proportion
is more readily seen.*
—Leonardo da Vinci

The Physical Properties Of The Pea Plant

Now, here's an interesting fact. Pea vines are elastic. When you decide to spend time in the beanstalks, they sometimes snap you right back into the pea patch. They aren't called snap peas for nothing, you know.

Each one of us has a different probability of change. How likely you are to change anything depends on:

> •how uncomfortable you are with the way things are now. If the level of discomfort isn't high enough, we let things stay the way they are. You may be acquainted with people in this situation. They talk about change a lot.
>
> •how attractive the future looks. Chances are you won't change if you're unclear about what you're changing to.
>
> •how successful you have been in the past at changing. How many times have you successfully broken a long-standing habit, stayed with something different and new through the long haul?
>
> •how much support you have for changing. Are the significant people in your life behind you on this change, or would they like you to stay just as you are?

Any one of these four factors can keep you just where you are. That's not bad. But if you want to be out of the pea vines, it's frustrating.

Any one of the four factors on the previous page can snap you back to your *current reality*. It's like you're inside a giant rubber band, stretching that rubber band as far as it can go.

And when you're not uncomfortable enough, when you lack a vision, when your history of successful changes is slight, or when you have no support, that rubber band will snap right back to it's original shape and size–and you'll snap back to just where you are right now.

INCREASING THE CHANCES OF CHANGE

Without knowing it, you've already got a good start. You know about timewasting, and doing it now. You recognize how stress can affect your energy and use of time. (You probably never knew procrastination and stress grew in the garden!)

You'll be even more successful if you talk out loud about changing. If you make verbal or written contracts with yourself, you're even more likely to make change happen.

When you hear hoofbeats in Texas, think of horses, not zebras.
—MEDICAL SCHOOL APHORISM

Patterns are not easy to see

Being able to recognize patterns in my life is like trying to see an entire iceberg. It rarely happens. Because most of the iceberg is hidden beneath the surface of the water.

The events in my life are the *tip* of the iceberg, the part that's easy to see. What's below the surface are the patterns and behaviors that shape my life. They're practically hidden and may cause events to occur and reoccur.

CHANGING EVENTS DOESN'T CHANGE BEHAVIOR

Look beyond events to patterns and behaviors that occur again and again, and you'll have a better chance at finding time for what's important in your life.

But it's got to be perfect!

Read this page only if perfectionism is your middle name.

Some of us confuse being successful with doing things perfectly. The two are not the same. They're from different places in the garden, and I think you know where.

Who says it's got to be perfect? Will the sky fall if it's not? Isn't it more likely that if you are an addicted perfectionist, you'll simply spend more time and energy doing something that may not warrant that kind of investment at all?

H. L. Mencken was right when he said that Puritanism is the haunting fear that somewhere, someone must be happy, but perfectionism has to be the fear that someone, somewhere, will find out that you're less than perfect all the time.

The Good News

People already know you're not perfect.

Working toward perfection is a sure way to build stress into your life. There is a point in every project, every argument, every endeavor, every communication, when we should be able to say *That's enough.*

And then let it go.

> *It doesn't have to be.
> It only has to look like it is.*

BUSY, BUSY, BUSY

Maybe you've gotten too used to what you think you should be doing? Why, what would happen if you didn't look harried, overworked, very busy! For some of us, the answer is—we probably wouldn't be recognized!

Maybe if I didn't look harried, I could look serene. I could appear calm, together, and happy. And this would be a bad thing? No, this would be a good thing. This would be time in the beanstalks.

Maybe if you didn't look overworked and stressed, you'd look approachable. Maybe friends would call more frequently, drop in, knock on your office door and ask you to take a coffee break with them.

> *Just because we have minds,*
> *doesn't mean we know how to operate them.*
>
> –Daniel M. Wegner
> White Bears and Other Unwanted Thoughts

Sometimes I make the choice not to bother busy people I know. I don't want to add more to their obviously complex lives. Perhaps people make the same choice concerning me.

People don't know you'd prefer their company. All they know is you look busy. This is not what Sherri Pryor calls making a memory. At least, it's not one you'd want to keep.

Control–it's not a bad thing.

It's a good thing. Once you recognize you *can* control your use of time, you own it. If your time seems out of control right now–have you given that control away? You have if you hear yourself saying:

- ❖ I have too much to do.
- ❖ I'll never get through this.
- ❖ I never have the chance to . . .
- ❖ There just aren't enough hours in the day.

All of those roughly translate to *I think I'll declare my lack of control. And if I can't control my time, well then it's not my fault if something never gets done. Is it?*

Well, who's responsible for putting jelly on your bread anyway? Are you willing to let someone else do that? Are you willing to let someone else decide how you'll use your time and energy?

Control Begins With You
You can't control the length of your life,
but you can control how you use it.
You can't control your facial appearance,
but you can control its expression.
You can't control another's opportunities,
but you can make your own.
You can't control the weather, but you can control
the moral atmosphere that surrounds you.
You can't control the attitudes of other people,
but you can make sure
that you always say "thanks"
and leave with a smile on your face.
You can't control the other fellow's
annoying faults, but you can see to it
that you do not develop similar faults.
Why worry about things you can't control?
Get busy controlling the things that depend on YOU.

*One of the symptoms
of an approaching nervous breakdown
is the belief that one's work
is terribly important.*
           —BERTRAND RUSSELL

Feeling in control of your life and your time is very different from wanting or needing A LOT OF CONTROL. One decreases stress, the other is a surefire stress builder.

The problem comes when control is your focus. Stephen Covey explains it well with his metaphor of the Circle of Influence and the Circle of Concern.

Here's a good book.

Connections
Quadrant II Time Management
by A. Roger Merrill

It's a classic. It will keep you in the beanstalks
and in the right circles.

❖ 5 ❖

The Fifth
Jelly Principle

AND WHAT HAPPENS IF YOU DO.
PUT YOUR ENERGY INTO THE THINGS
THAT GIVE YOU RESULTS.

Jelly Principle #1
Once you miss the first buttonhole,
you will have trouble buttoning up.

Jelly Principle #2
Someday is not a day of the week.

Jelly Principle #3
Time flies like an arrow.
Fruit flies like a banana.

Jelly Principle #4
If you are going to kill giants,
you must spend your time
in the beanstalks,
not in the pea vines.

Jelly Principle #5
Eat the big frogs first.

Now, listen up! As Calvin Trillen says, this is a great idea. And I don't have them that often. So pay attention!

> SOMETIMES THERE IS NO TIME.
> SOMETIMES THE BREAD LANDS
> JELLY SIDE ON THE CARPET.
> BECAUSE YOU DIDN'T PROTECT YOUR TIME.
> AND THEN YOU'VE GOT A CRISIS.

 THE GOOD NEWS
THE BAD NEWS
___

Big frogs must be eaten first, but they aren't necessarily appetizing.

Without a first course of big frog, I can find myself saying, *Yes, I planned to . . . but then . . . I probably should have done that right away . . .*

❖

*If you have to eat a frog,
don't look at it too long.*
—MARK TWAIN

The important things in your life have good manners. They don't shout, they're not rude. They're quiet, polite, and patient. They make no noise, even if you never get around to working on them. They wait, while your energy and attention are focused on less important things, while you're attending to the crisis du jour or today's squeaky wheel.

Parkinson's Law

Work expands to fill the time allotted to it.

Pryor's Law

Put your energy into the things that give you results.

Often the most important things in your life require you to eat the big frog first. That big frog may come disguised as a big step, a time consuming activity, something that takes research and coordination, something that requires planning or solitude. Frequently it seems so big, we pass on the first course.

The critical few and the trivial many

There's a vital concept in personal life management called *the critical few and the trivial many.* Guess which encompasses your important priorities? Guess where many people easily spend most of their time and energy?

The *critical few* are the things that make the most difference. The *trivial many* are the things that clamor for your time, attention, and energy.

In management and business, it's called the Pareto Principle or the 80/20 Rule.

> *A typical pattern will show that 80 percent of outputs result from 20 percent of inputs; that 80 percent of consequences flow from 20 percent of causes; or that 80 percent of results come from 20 percent of effort. The few things that work fantastically well, should be identified, cultivated, nurtured and multiplied.*
> —RICHARD KOCH
> THE 80/20 PRINCIPLE

As Price Pritchett says in his book *Fast Growth,* A few things are important, most are not.

According to common folk wisdom, if you put a frog into a pot of water the same temperature as his own, the frog will sit in the water even as the temperature of the water is raised. Perhaps it's the gradual change, but the water is dangerously hot when the frog finally discovers that fact.

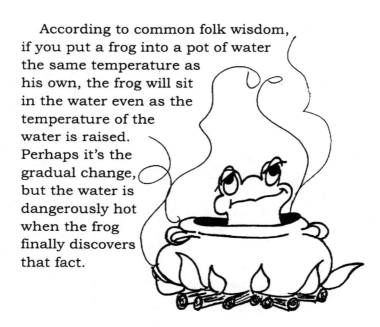

When your time isn't protected, you're as vulnerable as the frog in the pot. The water gets warmer, but it's not warm enough yet to move you to action. You may have the intention of doing something, should the water get too hot, but intentions aren't action.

My desk is covered with good intentions.
—BECKY GREEN

The best intentions, just like procrastination and worry, merely tie up energy. They don't protect your time. Eating big frogs first does. It keeps priorities from being shoved to the back burner. It keeps you sane, even with a million things to do. It gives you a feeling of control, energy, and maybe even success.

You can't stop the waves, but you can learn to surf.

*The important thing is this:
To be able at any moment to sacrifice
what we are for what we could become.*
—Charles Du Bois

When I'm thinking of eating a big frog, some good excuse usually comes to mind. Often, it's some remark starting with *But* . . .

The True Definition

BUT IS THE ACRONYM FOR
BEHOLD THE UNDERLYING TRUTH

Frequently featured in sentences beginning *Yes, but...* this particular conjunction provides a socially acceptable way of announcing my real intentions and my best excuses. It provides a hedge—one that has nothing to do with landscaping. It has, however, a lot to do with the landscaping of my life.

Living in the middle of Oklahoma is a windy, hot experience for a large part of the year. I love to garden, and I'd love for my garden to rival Martha Stewart's.

But she doesn't fight the Oklahoma wind.
It's not as hot there.
She has so much help.
You never see her mistakes.

And so for a long time, I didn't try, and my garden didn't have a chance to look like Martha Stewart's.

If you keep on saying
things are going to be bad,
you have a good chance of being a prophet.
—Isaac Singer

What I'd been saying is *I could have a garden like Martha's if . . .* and that's just a crafty way of rolling out my best excuses.

I needed to eat my big frogs first. My big frogs have been composting, windbreaking, seed babysitting, research, reading and planning. Not always tasty.

My garden probably never will look exactly like Martha Stewart's. That's all right. I like what I've done. I've tried some things I thought would never work. I've planted seeds that took three weeks to come up and six weeks before you could easily see them. And I'm closer to that pretty garden in my mind.

What happens if you don't eat the big frogs first? Nothing, absolutely nothing. At least for a while.

But if you begin to notice over time that some of your problems keep happening again and again, it's probably because you didn't eat the big frogs first.

You may find your energy tied up, your performance decreased, your stress level higher, and your health ultimately in danger.

It takes energy to find time for what's important in your life. It takes energy to move beyond *but*. Focus that energy on the things that give you results.

Look closely at what you wish was different, better, improved, more in place.

And ask yourself a very hard question:

Why isn't it?

Maybe even take the radical step of writing the answers down. And then find a word or phrase that describes each answer. Constancy, approval, harmony, opinions of others, fear of failing, lack of resources. I imagine most of your answers might fall under very few categories! Naming something often makes it manageable. Maybe even makes it palatable.

Life is a great big canvas, throw all the paint on it you can.
—DANNY KAYE

An excellent way to avoid eating big frogs first

Just create a crisis. It works every time. It carries great benefits. You get to be in the spotlight, the attention is great, sympathy pours in, you get a reprieve from doing what you should be doing, someone else may do the work for you.

Effective, but not recommended. Not if you want to find time for what's important in your life. If it keeps you from your goal, and creating a crisis does, it's not where your energy should be invested.

You don't have to be the bride at every wedding or the corpse at every funeral.

Time for a small reminder. Yes, I know you know all of this. Ahem, excuse me. Knowing is not doing. Remember?

It's easy to know. Knowing is passive. As in *I'll pass*, or *just pass it on*.

I know a lot. Especially about what I should do. So do I do it? Well . . .

Sometimes yes, sometimes no. Because doing requires action, motion, emotion, energy, decisions, choices, work, focus, and sometimes doing unpleasant things first. Makes me tired just to write that.

One by one, none of those are that hard, usually. However, if you are working, deciding, staying focused, you're expending a lot of energy with maybe nothing to show for it in the short term. *And because the results aren't immediate*, it's easy to say, *Oh, I know that.* So much easier than working now and seeing results a little later!

If knowing was doing, then I'd be trimmer, fit, have better relationships, be doing the boss's job!

I know how to fix balanced meals. I know about balancing flavors, textures, colors. I know the Food Pyramid, my nutritional requirements, and how to present food attractively.

You might have trouble seeing all this knowledge on display though, should you watch Mary J. Pryor prepare some of her meals.

For a lot of reasons, you might observe some of the following meals I've prepared:

A Tomato
(that's it, the whole meal)

Ice Cream
(straight from the box)

Ice Cream and Potato Chips
(a two course meal)

So much for the Food Pyramid! The plain fact is I know how to prepare delicious nutritious meals, but that doesn't mean I do it.

It's the same for finding time for what's important in your life.

You may think a tomato isn't a meal. Well tonight it was, because I was just too tired to fix anything else.

Was that the real reason? Maybe I was just too tired to fix anything else because I never focused during the day on getting the important things done. Maybe I got up late, rushed to get to work, got pulled off task a lot more than once, and the rest of the message . . .

*I used my energy
for things of little importance to me.*

Find is an action verb. That's why finding time for what's important to you means taking action.

How to eat a big frog:
- ❖ break it into smaller pieces.
- ❖ ask others for advice.
- ❖ write the week's priorities.
- ❖ do at least part of them.
- ❖ get better at what you do a lot of.

*Frogs have it easy.
They can eat what bugs them.*
—Council Bluffs Nonpareil

❖ 6 ❖

The Sixth
Jelly Principle

> **If your head
> is wax,
> don't walk in the sun.**
> —Ben Franklin

Leave Yourself Open To The Possibilities.

Jelly Principle #1
Once you miss the first buttonhole,
you will have trouble buttoning up.

Jelly Principle #2
Someday is not a day of the week.

Jelly Principle #3
Time flies like an arrow.
Fruit flies like a banana.

Jelly Principle #4
If you are going to kill giants,
you must spend your time
in the beanstalks,
not in the pea vines.

Jelly Principle #5
Eat the big frogs first.

Jelly Principle #6
If your head is wax,
don't walk in the sun.

It's time for review . . .

In business, people take time to review past accomplishments. Well, at least they do in smart businesses. They actually list their successes. But that's only part of the strategy. They also pay attention to goal direction, focus, and roadblocks that may be in their way.

Heads made of wax fall into the category of roadblocks. The biggest roadblocks to your success actually are the ones in that space between your ears. Sometimes it's not creative avoidance or lack of a vision that keeps us from our success. Sometimes it's our certainty that we already know everything we need to know. *I've made up my mind. Don't bother me with the facts!*

Ben Franklin had it right. If you're sure you know all the facts, sure you have the obviously correct course of action, stay out of the sun! Convince yourself you have all the answers and you're blocked. When you lock in to one way of thinking you usually lock out other potentially good ideas now or in the future.

> *There is a microscopically thin line*
> *between being brilliantly creative*
> *and acting like the most gigantic idiot on earth.*
> *So what the hell, leap.*
> —Cynthia Heimel

Leave yourself open to the possibilities!
Those possibilities are easier to discern when you know what you've accomplished so far. And no, it's not bragging. I didn't ask you to do this in front of a crowd. I'm just asking that you do it!

What have you done so far, toward finding time for what's important in your life? If it's easier, think of the week's accomplishments, or the month's. Just do it!

A distinguished author once used this quotation:

*The palest ink
is better than the best memory.*

Good advice. Write things down, because it's from your list of successes that you get the clearest picture of what work still has to be done. And it's hard to argue against your own evidence.

*Here is the test to find
whether your mission on earth is finished.
If you're alive, it isn't.*
—RICHARD BACH

You actually recognize more solutions to situations once you've talked to yourself. It's like you've given your mind permission to go into automatic search mode.

Ben Franklin's advice is for those who skip this step. By not analyzing where you are, you create a *scotoma*, a blind spot. You lock on to one way of thinking and doing things. You lock out any possibilities for change.

The Swiss lost the market for digital quartz watches because of a blind spot toward what they considered an insignificant market trend. In 1968 at the Watchmakers Annual Congress, the Swiss were not impressed by the digital watch. They didn't take the technology seriously, didn't even apply for a patent. Companies like Seiko however, were open to the possibilities.

Locking out the possibility that digital timepieces could ever be profitable cost 55,000 Swiss workers their jobs when manufacturing plants closed. The Swiss had erected a barrier for no other reason than they saw no reason to change! They knew what they were doing. They'd been the world's leader in watchmaking for centuries!

Hmmm . . .

Even the founder of IBM, Thomas Watson, said in 1970 that the world would only need ten computers. Fortunately, Watson was not locked on to that idea.

Leave yourself open to the possibilities. The recipe said it made ten servings. Kitty only wanted one bowl of soup. She started to pour the contents of the saucepan into ten bowls. Only then did it occur to her that there was a better way . . .

Who?

Who are you?

Who are you to think?

Who are you to think that?

Who are you to think that you can?

Who are you to think that you can change?

Who are you to think that you can change

the world?

Keep your thoughts positive,

Thoughts become your words.

Keep your words positive,

Words become your behaviors.

Keep your behaviors positive,

Behaviors become your habits.

Keep your habits positive,

Habits become your values.

Keep your values positive,

Values become your destiny.

—Gandhi

Lighten Up-Enjoy the Trip

Four bugs a day.

That's what my sister told me. Everybody needs four bugs a day. She'd read it, and wondered at the wisdom of that advice. Then she slowly realized she'd read it differently. Not wrong, differently. The article said everybody needed four *hugs* a day. We still laugh about that.

Tricia is sure enough of herself to tell other people this story and hear them laugh too, if they like. What she *should* have read doesn't bother her. The last thing you need to think about is the reaction of others to your priorities.

This doesn't equate with not caring about others. This addresses your right to see things your way.

Restructuring your priorities may get funny looks from some people. People might comment, criticize, laugh, raise an eyebrow. But that's where they are. That's not where you are. You're moving closer to where you want to be. Closer to having the time for what's important in your life. Besides, they are probably three bugs short for the day!

Leave yourself open to the possibilities.

Don't Do The Shoulds

If you're still bothered with a nagging voice saying *all this is good, but I should be doing . . .* Reread this book now!

What are your shoulds? You're on a first name basis with them. You *should* be able to quickly bring them to mind!

If not, separate things into the following columns. You'll recognize your shoulds–they will all be in Column Three. Throw away that column.

Have to	Want to	Don't have to

Be what you wish to seem.
—SOCRATES

Abandoning the shoulds is a good start. Abandoning anything that's outdated is another possibility. It's a strategy called *planned abandonment* and it's useful to uncover things already in place that no longer need to be.

> *Besides, some of the stuff that's been eating up*
> *your time and energy deserves to starve.*
> *Its all the clutter you've let creep into your life that*
> *really doesn't contribute anything to your future.*
> *It's the diddley routines you follow out of habit.*
> *And it's the urgent but trivial gunk*
> *that nags at you for attention,*
> *yet gives you nothing to help you grow.*
> —PRICE PRITCHETT

What are the things you would *not* start doing today if you weren't already doing them?

> *It is a common experience*
> *that a problem difficult at night*
> *is resolved in the morning*
> *after the committee of sleep has worked on it.*
> —JOHN STEINBECK

Jelly Side Up is just a way—

It's not rocket science. It won't make or wreck world peace. But it may increase your sense of peace.

Instead of feeling hesitant or unsure—feel good about finding time for what's important in your life, regardless of the response it gets.

In a speech to the American Society for Training and Development, Dr. Ann McGee-Cooper talked about her desire to learn tap dancing and deciding to do just that, after she'd turned 50. When she went to the dance store for tap shoes, the clerk's question was, "And how old is the little girl?"

"Fifty two," she said. She laughed, and so did her audience.

The average six-year-old kid
laughs 300 times a day.
The average adult
laughs only between 15 and 100 times a day.
Studies show that laughing
decreases the level of stress hormones and
strengthens the immune system.
—Dr. Lee Berk

Add Joy To Your Daily Life

Pay as much attention to the things that are

working positively in your life as you do

to those that are giving you trouble.

Rake a big pile of leaves every fall

and jump in it with someone you love.

Memorize your favorite love poem.

Learn three knock knock jokes so you will

always be ready to entertain children.

Don't let weeds grow around your dreams.

Remember that everyone you meet

is afraid of something, loves something,

and has lost something.

Regardless of the situation, react with class.

Let some things remain mysterious.

—H. Jackson Brown, Jr.
Life's Little Instruction Book, Volume II

Leave yourself open to the possibilities.

The Obituary
I Don't Want To Never See

Mary J. Pryor died suddenly and unexpectedly at the age of 49 years, 9 months, and 28 days. She will be missed. Mary's friends remember her as always busy, and very, very dedicated to her work. No matter how much she had to do, Mary took it all seriously. She worked nights and weekends, and was never known to leave things undone. She had a high standard and held herself to it.

She could work almost anybody under the table and often did. Because she was so reliable, many people came to her with problems for which she accepted responsibility.

Although she frequently suffered chest pains, Mary often told people that she knew how to manage stress.

After all, she gave workshops on the subject.

The family requests memorials to Habitat for Humanity, Compassionate Hands, or Yukon's Pets and People. These were the organizations Mary believed in and had planned on supporting, after she stopped working at such a stressful pace.

She is survived by her husband Jack, and by her cats–TC, Pumpkin and Charlie, whom she took little time for, because work always came before play.

Mary loved to garden, although in the last ten years she had little time to enjoy what she once hoped would be the prettiest place in Canadian County.

❖❖❖

You can easily understand why I never want to see that piece of news. If I leave myself open to the possibilities however, I should be able to rest in peace. My priorities will have been worked and lived, not discussed and never used.

Leave yourself open to the possibilities!

Jim Carrey imagined success all his life.

In 1990, before that success was evident, he wrote a check to himself for ten million dollars. Noting that it was for "acting services rendered," he postdated it Thanksgiving, 1995. When that time came, Carrey's movie roles had already earned him much more than ten million dollars.

Man must sit in chair
with mouth open
for very long time
before roast duck fly in.
—ANCIENT CHINESE PROVERB

❖ 7 ❖

First Aid
For Jelly Down Days

So many projects, resolutions, and dreams never make it. And that's too bad, because that means we can say–true or not–*Well, I've tried that, and I'll tell you, it just didn't work.*

What an individual may be saying is:

I tried too much at once.

I looked at what I thought was the problem but it was just a symptom of the problem.

I spread myself too thin.

Now this is a sticky subject, like jelly. Like jelly, that's not all bad.

It Bears Repeating

Don't get the guilts.

It is NOT the intent of this book to make you guilty about choices you've made. Jelly Side Up! is just a tool to help you think about your choices.

Flexibility
means doing what works this week.

Twelve Step Programs use a saying all of us could benefit from:

I did the best I could
with the information I had at the time.

And we do. Today we might make different choices, but we're different people today. When you recall decisions that aren't ones you'd include in your resume, don't waste time and energy on the guilts. Think instead of all you've learned! From all your experiences!

Doubting that your past choices contained anything to learn from? Think again. How about better judgement? How about patience? How about the long view?

So give yourself some credit, and spread it thickly!

Use Your Gifts

In *Living Juicy*, SARK explains some unique properties of gifts.

> *. . . continuing to have excuses, not feeling challenged, having a ready explanation for not living our dreams, having more "time," basking in the glow of denial.*
>
> *These "gifts" will continue to feed areas of low self-esteem until you believe in your own abilities to fly.*

More First Aid
Learn To Receive

Speaking of giving, most of us are very good at it. So good, that we find it hard to let someone give to us.

Susan had waited a long time for her Yorkie puppy. Three weeks after the dog arrived, her husband's respiratory problems led to the decision that Star would be given to a friend.

When tests indicated that a puppy at home made no difference to Frank's health, Susan was overjoyed.

As happy as she was when the puppy came back home, "I felt bad," she said. "Harry brought Star back before we'd even asked. Then he assured us he'd care for her whenever we needed him to, like whenever we'd be gone on vacation. But we're so used to giving, *I caught myself feeling bad about that.* I realized I was in the receiving position, and that wasn't a comfortable feeling for me."

> *What we have to learn to do, we learn by doing.*
> —Aristotle

Your mind is a wonderful, powerful tool. Why is it that we can put so much faith in computers? in the Postal Service? in the space program? in television advertisements? in what others think and promise? And yet, when it comes to believing our own best source, we doubt all that accumulated experience, all that wisdom, all that power *just waiting to be used.*

Don't get the guilts. Use your gifts. Learn from them. Learn to receive.

A hidden belief

that many of us hold is that

there is something wrong with being too happy.

We have been taught that it's arrogant

to think we're deserving of total happiness.

If anything comes into our lives—love, success,

happiness—which seems like it would be suited

to a 'deserving' person,

we conclude it can't possibly be for us.

We have been unable to accept joy

because it doesn't match who we think we are,

yet it is not only our right, but in a way,

our responsibility to be happy.

—MARIANNE WILLIAMSON
A RETURN TO LOVE

Even More First Aid For Jelly Down Days

PUSH FOR ORGANIZATION

Jelly down days are bad enough. They need no help from us. The more focus you can muster on those bad days, the more you'll feel like you control the direction of your life. Being organized is *not* a disease, it's a habit or a practice that can give you results.

Take a lesson from Stacie, Susan's then eleven-year-old daughter. Like most girls her age, Stacie's highest priorities don't always include straightening up her room, getting homework done first. You know, those things parents think of as somewhat important. Stacie's relaxed attitude can change drastically when she's focused on a goal. The more important it is, the more she organizes and plans.

For a class field trip that required a sack lunch, Stacie left Susan a note. That alone was not a usual occurrence. Actually, she left more than a note. Now, Susan is a good mother and doesn't require detailed instructions. But this was important to Stacie. She organized and communicated as clearly as she could. She covered all the bases. She left no loopholes. She got results.

Stacie's List

Stacie Lunch

Pringles	BBQ
Sandwich	Peanut but + Jelly
Peanuts	Dry Roasted
Jell-o	Chocolate with vanilla swirl
Water	In the fl— cup — see →
Spoon	plastic

Here's a good book.

Living Juicy
Daily Morsels for Your Creative Soul
by SARK

As SARK herself says—I believe that we are each highly creative with important gifts to share, words to speak and write, lights to shine on ourselves and others.

Here's another one!

Start Now!
Life Is Too Short
by Mary J. Pryor

A book to inspire you, to move you off of dead center, to convince you to start living your dreams now.

Almost Final Advice

*He who cannot rest, cannot work;
he who cannot let go, cannot hold on;
he who cannot find footing, cannot go forward.*
—Harry Emerson Fosdick

A famous* author once asked,

What are you waiting for?

and she's asking it again.

What are you waiting for?
your mother's permission?
your children's approval?
your colleagues' full support and understanding?
a truckload of courage?
sharper pencils?
better clothes?
newer paints?
a more opportune time?
more time to practice?
a little time to prepare?
a lot of time to prepare?
some time to think about it?
—Mary J. Pryor

* See page 48. You are entitled to your own opinions.

The clocks in my house
all tick in disparate rhythms,
but the time they keep
goes forward.

Someday
you will realize
that you are not waiting
for life to begin.
This is your life.
—Joyce Carol Oates

The End

About Mary J. Pryor

Mary is an award-winning writer, speaker, and video producer.

She is a skilled communicator who gets her point across with humor and a human touch.

Mary's first book, *Start Now! Life Is Too Short,* is in its second printing. Its companion piece, *Life Is Too Short–More Inspiration on the Subject* will be available in 1998.

She's a member of the National Speakers Association and a founding member of the Pryor Group–a company dedicated to building people personally and professionally through training in motivation, communication, planning, and goal setting.

Let Mary inspire and motivate you. Her customized programs deliver the message in creative exciting ways.

For more information, call (405) 354-1604
or write to
Mary J. Pryor
P.O. Box 851435
Yukon, Oklahoma 73085-1435
pryorgp@icnet.net